Pomegranate Wine

Pomegranate Wine

Poems by Arlene Swift Jones

Turning Point

Published by Turning Point
P.O. Box 541106
Cincinnati, OH 45254-1106

Typeset in Galliard by WordTech Communications LLC, Cincinnati, OH

ISBN: 1933456116
LCCN: 2005908454

Poetry Editor: Kevin Walzer
Business Editor: Lori Jareo

Visit us on the web at www.turningpointbooks.com

Acknowledgments

Grateful acknowledgment is given to the editors and publishers of the following in which some of these poems first appeared:

Andrew Mountain Press (Chapbook): "Edward Hopper's Girlie Show, 1940's," "Going Home to Iowa," "Silences," "Symbiosis"

Calyx: Women And Aging: "Rheumatoid Arthritis," "Country Hospital," "Vintage"

Chicory Blue Press: A Wider Giving: "Lumbar Fusion," "With Apologies to Blake and Exxon"

Cimarron Review: "Svetlana Alliluyeva: On Her Father"

Crone's Nest: "Martha"

The Denny Poems: "Madonna del Parto"

Green Mountains Review: "If Only I Had Never Gone to Evora," "Saint's Relics"

Iowa Woman: "The Return of Canada Geese..."

Kalliope: "Mater Dolorosa"

Kansas Quarterly: "Red Cabbage" published as "The Cabbage Sphere"

Kestrel: "Madonna della Misericordia," "Apple of My Eye," "Madonna of the Pomegranate," "The Tomato," "De Humani Corporis Fabrica"

Long Pond Review: "George Sand to Frederic Chopin, in Majorca"

Prairie Schooner: "Piazza Navona in Summer"

Sojourner: "Mother: Daughter"

Tar River Poetry: "Poussin's Martyrdom of St. Erasmus"

I wish to acknowledge the help and support I have been given by friends/teachers and by foundations whose belief in me has given me courage:

The MacDowell Colony, The Ragdale Foundation (which honored me with the Frances Shaw Fellowship for older women writers), Warren Wilson MFA for writers and the many distinguished teachers and students who were present. Particularly among them, Eleanor Wilner, whose clear-eyed intelligence, generosity, and enormous humanity are an example to all writers. I wish to thank Nancy Krim, fellow student at Warren Wilson for her support and her editing. And I wish to thank Dick Allen, mentor, friend for his generous support.

*This book is lovingly dedicated to my three daughters
and their father*

Contents

I. White Cone Heart

Red Cabbage

I cut the red cabbage.
The sharp blade unfolds
layer after layer

pushed together, fold
after rolling fold of white,
purple-coated leaves.

They bleed on my fingers
or do my fingers bleed
dark bluish blood

upon the cabbage?
The slicer whines
against my hand.

Layers open: thickening
and thinning, branching out
from the tough, inedible,
white cone heart.

De Humani Corporis Fabrica, The Fifth Book: Female Generative Organs Andreas Vesalius, 1543

I was not nobly born, and I was held in disrepute
because Brother Giovanni, of the order of St. Anthony,
called *Il Santo* in Padua, was my lover.
I carried his child in my womb.
Oh, why had he taken Orders?

My parents and my lover came to my grave
with flowers and a crucifix to find my body gone.
Outraged at such defilement, such blasphemy,
they took my case to city magistrates.
But they could not find my corpse: Vesalius
and his students skinned and dismembered me,
so no one could know whose body it had been.

I was stolen from the tomb
by Andreas Vesalius, body snatcher and anatomist.
Never was I so beheld while I lived,
with such nervous, rapt attention.
No one, not even Giovanni, had seen my body naked.
How they carved it. They took out my heart,
my organs, my little child, they drew pictures
as though they were Giotto, or Cimabue.
I heard them laugh, I heard them wonder
if they'd find the devil when they touched
what would have been a child of sin.
But they touched him, cut him out.

Oh, St. Anthony, make my body whole,
put it back into my grave, my little nest
of eggs, the swimming sperm like kisses
to my dark mouth.

Rheumatoid Arthritis

for Drs. CLC, CSR at *The Hospital for Special Surgery*, NYC

Parts of my hands, my left
knee, are dust. They were
incinerated in the hospital
dump. Ashes already.

We work together, decide
which bones have expired
their use, talk about them
like old friends now dis-

tanced by their going off.
Now the shoulders' turn: their
sockets once gleaming remark-
ably like giant pearls

in their oyster cases,
the bluebone now bruising
as beachstones with the sea
gone, leeched away. Its

synovial sheath corroded, it
scrapes the pearl metamorphosed
into sponge gone fossil-rigid.
We talk about them as though

they are a raspberry garden
brambled by overgrowth, by
canes which must be thinned
to save the strength of berries,

to fatten the purpling mass,
sweeten juices; as though they
are bittersweet gone beyond
into a neighbor's orchard,

climbing trees, choking apples.
It is better to lose parts
bit by bit than have the earth
greet you whole, and suddenly.

The Operation

They brought *Betadine* in a paper cup:
disinfecting, the stain
yellowed my skin. They punctured
my bluest vein: ungracious, bare,
the IV waited to do its job.
Through halls of perfidious tumors
waiting patiently to be excised
they wheeled me to doors
which said *No entry*
beyond this point! Shivering
in stained skin, under a worn gown's
faded geometric flowers
I entered a dazzling arena;
I was lifted to its chilled stage.

Eyes peered from green gauze helmets,
muffled voices drummed my ears
with words that weren't for me:
all the mysteries of my body
yielded up to them:
my only part was presence.

I awake into a room
abandoned by language, empty
of cool hands to say *It's over.*
No curtain calls for me
nor in the crowded space
is there a place for flowers.

In this room the bell I ring
is never answered.

Intensive Care

Only white coats enter this landscape
wearing masks for faces, faces without words
for us: this is a wordless place. Pain

tells us we are alive: we cherish it.
Under the drownings of needles, the suck-
ing tubes, our green hearts

jump on the TV screen—thrillers
that occupy our minds. Familiar eyes
peer at us, expecting to see a map

of a new country on the outline
of a sheet, intrigued to know John's heart
was held by human hands.

The colostomy under the bedsheets
makes faces turn away, knowing
that hands unsnaked the knotted mass

of innards whose story the tube
from my nose tells, as it carries
the curdled waste of food

caught undigested. Henry's multi-
plying cells are unstopped,
careening drunkenly into the intricate

passages of his interiors… Faces cannot
        greet us, faces which saw last weeks'
flower petals fall as soundlessly

as thoughts outside this room.
We see the clouds fall, we see
the architecture of our careful dreams.

We see things you haven't seen.

Country Hospital

Row upon row of rooms contain us,
survivors of numerous small deaths:
burns, bones bracketed in steel,
breath fractured, blood
falling into confusion with itself.

Henry is next door. He has spent
his seven ages but still his chest
moves air that whispers
the lost sound of trees. The nurse
rustles in with instruments for ears

eyes that record but don't see.
Her stethoscope confirms our lifebeat
but some hearts dance
like madmen in her ears;
some sound faint as a pinfall.

Tom broke his leg—a meeting
with a stone too bare, too early for snow.
He wants out—his blood
paces his body's corridors
unspent it boils over. *Damn,* he swears.

Millie (we are first names only)
is out of ICU. Her hair forgot
what color it was. It is the stubble
left in the spring field. In front
of the morning window the wisps

are dazzled white as a star. Bare
limbs of the tree behind her
branch out of her head, one with
last leaves falling into winter.
Her hands are blue twigs holding

her face which is the color my eyes
give her, the color of nothing
fading. She faces me knees to
knees, a hall between us. Hers
that once were white, caressed,

are spotted with purple, her
legs show ropes of blood trying
to climb home. Sandy's adolescent
appendix nearly burst but didn't.
She is petulant and feels cheated

not to have felt danger, denied
the thrill of death that brushed
her by. Her diminished voice
she uses to make mothers cry.

We are rooms of hope standing
like ninepins. We want but do not
want to know who stands, who falls.

If Only I Had Never Gone to Evora...

If only I had never gone, I think, *to Evora...*

Down this long table of the wine
and garden roses, our eyes' dark opals
reflect the candle's fire.
A burning log takes away our chill

here in the country, oxidizing the fat
and lean circling years of this arbor
vitae log. Once it stood tall
in sheltering grace, at the entrance to the garden.

It is the autumn of us here, at this table,
where above the candlelight our mouths move,
moist, red, masticating the trivia
of the lives we cling to, our words diminished

and diminishing. I undress the opening lips,
empty the caverns of our eyes,
peel back the good and bad noses
to their hard elements: *If only*

I had never gone, I think, to Portugal,
to Evora, to the Baroque Chapel of The Bones
where walls are stacked-up femurs
and arches are made of round, hard skulls.

There, in Evora, I saw them: those skulls
of faith, the empty arms of bones.

Sol of the Body Brace Shop

Sol wrapped my stockinged body
in warm wet plaster gauzes,
my elbows akimbo

on a horizontal rod,
knees bent forward
to straighten my spine.

The plaster dried in minutes.
I felt dressed for combat,
stiff in armor.

But, zip
With a knife, Sol cut it
straight down the back

and eased me out...
Sol made a negative
out of my positive

from which he made
a fiber glass shell,
translucent, milky,

hard as a clam. I am
no crawling carapace or bug,
I'm a shiny creature

on legs, fastened
with velcro.
Sol makes me stand.

Vintage

—in the hospital

I have gone beyond the desire
   for a case of good wine
that you promised, my dear,
   if I ever get out of here,
disparaging, even insulting
   as I have been, not to your
tastes, but to your value
   of tastes, as you have measured
it, in hard cash. Currency
   outlives us, and endures.

   I am already into the new wine,
listening to the New World
   Symphony. Dvorak was once,
too, new to it all...
   Now it is my ears, my eyes
that hunger, more than my
   tongue thirsts, for a country
I have never explored:
   Homesickness and longing

are not currency for any
   endurance—no *place,* not
one inch of earth, one flower
   can promise that it loved me:
Earth's love was always un-
   requited.

Poussin's *The Martyrdom of St. Erasmus*

from the Vatican Exhibit at the Metropolitan Museum

The real crowdgatherer is
Poussin's bloody martyrdom
of Erasmus. His back on
a bench, his hands tied

to a block behind his head,
torso stretched drumtaut.
Attached to a rope a hook
obvious in its intent,

gouges inwards to innards
which will be pulled out
by a wheel. It will un-
ravel Erasmus: stomach

squashed, his intestines
will wrap like rope on
the spool. All will follow:
the hooked liver, the found

lungs bursting their air.
Erasmus's eyes are paired
agates circling the small
rooms of his skull: his

teeth grind the reddening
mouth. All watch:
the helmeted soldier,
the man at the wheel

to turn it, two angels
to place laurel
on his body. We, too, wait—
to catch the heart

still beat on the hook,
see the last silence sweep
the failed hands, the stilled feet.

The Sculptor' Hands

A woman sculptor smiles from the front page
of *The Register* in the good light of her face,
her short, shadow-catching hair,
her New England country costume—
a cotton turtle under wool cableknit.
I can tell it's wool by the way the cables lie
like deep earthbrown furrows rising
softly on either side. Her hands rest on her knees;
one hand gently in the other—hands I recognize,
with a wide wedding band and diamond ring
she can still wear on her left ring finger
even with the green-applebud swellings
of the third joints. The knobby right-hand fingers
curl around that hand. Her sculpture
of a figure emerging from stone doesn't know
the pain of a hand on the chisel, but I know
how her fingers are stiffened, how their movement
argues with pain.
                        In my lap fingers curl
and uncurl—my failed, antediluvian hands.

Sarajevo, October 1992

"Off to see your lady friend
again?" Adem's friends ask.
"She waits for me," he says...

The zoo in Sarajevo is silent.
Even the growl is gone
from the one remaining bear
who leans against her cage
to reach for bread from the hand
of Adem Hodzic. He thought he heard
a low sound from her throat,
but it was his hope he'd made
audible without knowing, or
the friction of his rifle
against the cartridge belt.
The dazed bear stumbles
through a landscape of ribcages;
she licks her mate's jawbone
matted with fur and some
remaining disintegrated flesh.
Weeks ago she ate his heart, his liver.

Adem covers his nose and mouth.

Considering

Out of a *Whirlpool* water will cleanse,
out of frost into fire, flesh will be roasted,
bread will be baked and we shall break it
and eat together on a slab of granite stone
in my new kitchen (half-way from Albany
to Hartford on Route 44) with *Gaggenau*
and *Hofstra*, hardware that will outlive us
and our kitchens.
                           I wash purple grapes
that glow with a dark moon's whiteness,
I hear public radio's story—two Muslim men
survived the Serb execution of 200 men,
half of them boys, on the edge of a ravine.
Bodies thudded down on them thick as rain,
heavy as boulders—their fathers, sons.
They were down there.
They tell their stories.
                           On my table
TIME lies open to Pamela Bashu's dark beauty,
before her face was scraped away from her.
Dragged behind her own pale gold BMW
her body was shredded away from her bones.

I stand in my BMW of kitchens, gagging now,
watching the car-thief murderers, one 16 years,
blow kisses to a female officer
at their arraignment.
                           Come to my aid, God,
here in my kitchen (To be ignorant of evil

is not to be innocent).

Consider the lilies Yourself, God:
I have followed the venal mood:
I have consumed, I consume—
consuming is a responsibility.
I have not walked with You,
in the valley, the town,
or on any hill, because I fear shadows.

I fear the absence of Your presence.

I fear Your presence.

Laments from the Holy Land

Taraneh, come away from the well.
We will drink wine....
Because you ran
the sniper saw you.
Shoot anything that moves.
For that your black hair
seeps red. For that—
but not only—
I blew myself up
in Jerusalem.

*

The earth consumes bodies
of generals, of soldiers.
But the innocents, oh
the innocents too
are massacred.
Why did you come back, Herod?

*

Rachel, you are afraid.
Take the children—
all children—
leave the parched ground,
seeded with venom, not stars.

*

Oh pomegranate tree,
your red juice mixes with our blood.
Oh so so red.

*

Joseph, tell the Pharoah
you want to stay in Egypt land.
Anyplace is better than here.

Joshua, maybe you fought the battle of Jericho
but you have never seen anything
like this, how the dragons with steel arms
embrace us all.

*

Ahmed, you are so young,
so small, you cannot kill
the giant. Hate cannot die.

*

The horses of Krupp were black, belching fire.
The Polish horses were groomed
for their finest hour,
carried impeccable riders.
The end was quick.

*

Rows of little Davids are boys
throwing stones at tanks.
This happens in the promised land
where not one will ever become king.

Saints' Relics

In the last room before the exit
of the *Museo Civico* in Sansepolcro,
as a reminder that miracles can exist,
bone fragments of saints rest
in gold-leafed Florentine frames,
sealed under glass:

the third finger of San Feliciani;
a piece of San Fabiano's femur,
its frame on a pedestal—sealed in 1678
with faded ribbon and the red wax seal
of Bishop Lodovico, an expert in saints' bones;
the vertebrae of San Dometz
surrounded with *putti* wearing crowns;

a fragment of pelvis from Santa Modesti
next to a bit of San Germano's cranium,
San Aurelius' radius and
the noble second toe of San Juliani.
Angels guard the ulna of San Quirini
and sing the praises of Santa Theoduli's small elbow.

II. The Stem It Twists Upon

Chiaroscuro

I

The apple leans into the light.
From its pink-froth April opener,
it grows, greens, fattens,
turns and follows
in the sun's path,
burnishing its own shadow,
closing fiercely
around the star-shaped core.
Little cartilaginous chapels,
does the light find its way
to illuminate the seed within?
Are the five adjoining chambers
which make a star, kept dark,
the fruit smothering the seed?

II

In autumn, walking on fallen leaves,
I look up and see the sun
stellate on the leaves' gathering darkness—
rays of it, spread as brightness streams
through cracks, a lighthouse beaming outwards
from its great contained light—
until the rays are lost
in the greater blue above trees.

If I walked directly under
one of the rays
breaking starlike from the trees,
would it touch me?

But the light is silent,
shining out of its great
mute secret, like the silence
of my own heart
that does not tell me
if it sees ribs
like thick trunks of trees
sinuated into thinnest
purple-sunset branches
as it peers out
from its remotest chambers.

Madonna Del Parto

Piero della Francesca, c. 1453

1

"Take *la strada bianca*," they said,
—the white road—"until you come
to the cypresses." In Tuscany
bianca is the color of dust.
The road winds, narrow, white as bone.
Cypress trees lead the way,
their dark heads nod, beckoning;
they ring the dead. Perhaps they remember
a young man carrying paints
to a small chapel...
                          He left a young woman
standing alone, framed by a tent
held open by two village boys
with wings. Her dress is blue
as the rosemary flower—it is unbuttoned
where she swells in her ninth month....
Her left arm akimbo, the hand opens outwards,
cupping the darkness that rises from the folds
of her skirt. Her right hand
rests lightly on her taut belly
as though she had known all along
how big she would be, how ordinary.

Her face is quiet, pale as the sky
before sunrise, before this event
which would change the world...

What more could a young man
give to the dead than that they go
willingly to lie near her?

2

He didn't see me as they did—
the peasants of Monterchi—
just after I flowed from his brush:
a girl, flaunting pregnancy,
unashamed, unbuttoning my dress.

They stood smelling of cow manure
and the pigsty, awkward and whispering:

Why are her clothes from the cottage,
and the boys—if they are supposed
to be angels, why aren't they dazzling
in white, their wings lifted and shining
with gold leaf, instead of folded up,
the color of pigeons?
Why does the halo look like a breadloaf
if she is supposed to be our Madonna?

It was the tent where I stood
that arrested their eyes.
It rose—a lordly pavilion—
and I saw, even not looking at them,
how they thought its rosettes
were a great person's insignia.

Otherwise, I should have seemed

nothing to them, a body to whore with
had not someone got there first.

3

In Monterchi, in August, the watermelon
bellies forth. Wheat is long-harvested,
lavender seed has dropped into
a lacy shawl, a perfumed shadow.

Tiny *rosmarino* flowers
lighten dark pungent needles;
sunflowers stand in shop-green full skirts—
they are women on market day,
nodding and gossiping.

Zucchini burgeon under hairy broad leaves,
tomatoes turn brassy red—
their yellow seeds ooze a red jelly,
a confiture of sunlight.
Peaches in downy gold skin
hang like the breasts of the fruitpickers.

Pears are pendulant, the grapes massed
as honeycombs. Here is nothing
but ripeness, suspended, redolent.

Three things move silently:
a nearly imperceptible nod
from the beckoning cypresses;
the eye which must follow;
a young woman's hand
unbuttoning her dress.

Apple of My Eye

In Cyprus, sages told my little daughter
the enormous blister on her toe
was contamination from the fig tree
as old as Methuselah, they said,
cloaked and bearded clergy in a row
shaking heads with stovepipe hats,
five index fingers pointing up
to sheltering thick shade.
The smallest scratch will get infected!
And the blister won't get better
if she climbs that tree...
Mumbling, they added, *It was not*
your northern apple, but the fig!

I had already dreamed her there—
in the wide supporting branches
of the fig tree, standing in a house
of leaves—like giants' hands—
making shade for her, and proffering
the purple sweetness of a thousand
plummy seeds, hung pendulant,
in honey. No more a child, I saw
a woman with my daughter's cornsilk hair,
who wouldn't listen to advice
or reason any more than separate
her lithe and naked body from that tree.

Entwined within the leaves' dark shade
I saw the serpent, his shiny crested head

circling her, in spires—
I saw his chilling beauty
And watched the serpent's eye beguile.
From my tangled vine I saw
the craved-for fruit hanging from that tree.
He gazed at her that was my child:
I heard him say *You are resplendent!*
His eyes, like jewels, gazed at her insatiate.

Those graybeards knew their warning
wouldn't stop a child climbing barefoot
up the giant tree. They pulled
protruding necks inside dark cassock shells,
while she, ingrate daughter, never turned
her head to see her mother, waiting.

Silences

—for Tillie Olsen

There are graves all around me
      of poems.
They are my own.
      I have walked over them
An insult to the dead
      my mother said
to walk on graves.

      I walk on them.

They are untended—
      aborted—
      a tear in the grass.

My mother was right:
      the graveyard
walks, follows me
      everywhere
reminds me of hulls, husks
      skeletons, shells.

I have tried to fill
      that emptiness in me
with womanly things:
      jars of pickles
letters, cookbook meals.

The graves stalk me;
      the graves have eyes
      arms, legs
pickaxes, shovels;
      they would bury me.

Mother: Daughter

She hates my love
which defines her
as a compass
defines its circle.

Once so delineated
the circle
has its own life
and invented
in fact
the compass
which defines it.

Lacoön died
with his sons
entwined
by the serpent.

Is love too
a serpent
walking upright
as serpents did
before the Fall

thereafter
to make a circle
biting its own tail?

Mater Dolorosa

Mary, I know it was hard for you
  having to flee your country
        and then to find no room

at the inn
  only a stable
        Joseph angry

thinking you had tricked him
  maybe your donkey lame
        no one ever mentioned

you were probably hungry
  straw wasn't exactly bread
        maybe there was milk

from the cow
  if Joseph
        angry or not

would have milked her
  not to even mention
        running water

a basin bed
  but what if
        after all that

your baby asked you
 why the day came
            that he was born

and there was no way
 to undo
            what was done

stable or not
 and you really
            wanted to

After Botticelli's *Madonna of the Pomegranate*

The virgin is holding a pomegranate
in her right hand; the arm cradles
her infant. The pomegranate's
ruby seed-facets glisten
in the white hand
of the virgin. Against her blue cape
it is a red ball of sun
in the pale sky of morning.
The child has a golden arc
painted around his head.
The sky deepens to blue.

Pomegranate!
Your spilt red juice stains
mouths of lovers, their lips, fingers,
their white skin. Sated womb,
you grow big with hope.
My body, too, was once luscious,
pear-shaped, pendulant
as a purple fig, my navel
a round goblet, brimming.

The virgin has never changed:
her face still adores her child;
and the pomegranate is red forever;
the sky, unchanged, deep
in its blue. Lines on her face
are only cracks in the paint

on old wood—a warped panel.

My children have grown.
I do not hold them.
I wish we had stayed together
adored: adoring, my breath
remained the smell of apples
to my lover, my body
a continent for him alone
with the smell of trees
and rain and the earth's
furrows warm with heat.

Now you are dead,
old womb, dried pomegranate,
leathery as an empty wineskin,
this caved-in dome of heaven,
this shrunken sphere.

Saint Elmo's Fire

—In memory of my mother,
from Warsaw, 1960

Black crosses of Palmiry
stand in a wavering distance
from this broken city.
Its wounded citizens
need miracles.

I, too.

They see St. Elmo's fire
on the steeple of the one church which stands
amid the rubble
of Warsaw's crushed horizon.
They make nightly vigil,
they long for what they see:
corpos sanctum, the holy fire—
it lingers, vanishes, returns.
Half-believing, they believe
He is at last revealed,
descended, surely.

I cradle daughters
close to me and fiercely
but it is *your* hands that are
around them, moving surely
through the pathless ocean.

There is a deep cold sea between us
yet it is your face I see
high on that church steeple,
luminous and full of love

You lie afloat in satin,
white and tufted, cold as snow,
while the Ladies' Guild serves cake
and coffee to the mourners,
who ask of me—
the absent daughter.

I am across an ocean
wider than disbelief
where faces, upturned and longing
in this uncertain light
wear hope like wounds, unbandaged...

There is something here
that will not let me be,
moving fast, mysterious
like the steeple fire transmuted
under an icy ache of sea
unbearable: Leviathan—
his burning path
in darkest depths of me.

Martha

I am eighty-six. A thatch of bone.
Knees prominent. Elbows now kindling
that once were saplings—my skin
a paper birch. I am a cankered tree
stuck fast in dry earth, grounded.

But my thoughts are clouds.
I watch my daughters watch me,
they whisper how my mind goes wandering
in a lost universe, how I
talk to stars. Children, would you

stay at home in this haunted house?
Your mutterings are only rain
gusting through the summer screens
in Kansas City, or the wide Missouri
murmuring, no more to me than gossipings

of fallen leaves underfoot.
I, too, had flesh the color of spring,
of pink shells on a tawny beach,
my belly a tangle of roots nesting,
my lips a blur of rain.

I remember the sun and me
striding forth daily, passing
me on—one dance partner to another—
to the moon, a slight bow, stars
falling on their knees to me,

sleep I went to meet at dawn.
The rain will come and loosen
these mired feet, this cankered tree,
will let me flee. I'll go back,
       I'll glide on that wide river.

With Apologies To Blake And Exxon

Tiger, tiger, in your cool
night forest, come down out
of that burning bright
and fill my whatever-is-

the-equivalent of tank:
my sinews, my teeth...my nails,
to make me a burning
red dread. She-devil, if

you like. Come into my
smoldering and make my
brain, each innard flame.
No blame, my tiger.

I will be no lamb.
Burn me right up to the
last detail. In short,
immortalize my poetic

nights and in the day
just lay those velvety
strips and tawny touch
right over my symmetry.

Svetlana Alliluyeva: On Her Father, Joseph Stalin

His presence erased all other presences,
his voice drowned out all other voices.

My mother's voice grew quieter
and quieter and then was lost to me:
I ran through empty rooms
following its last faint throb
speaking to me, asking him for grace,
for her, for me…
What is grace, I wondered.

His eyes pinned me to corridors,
to brick, to stone, to staircases—
outside the walls
they looked like graceful towers.

I was swallowed by it
taking it for love. And then
I weakened. Who, I ask, would not, for love?
His appetite was for the world
and not for me—we were consumed
and then disgorged: his hunger
was insatiate.

He is spewed up now, outside walls
he stood upon in his dark stride,
and though I am disgorged
I turn and run, and run again.

I am still his kingdom.

The Islands

—in memory of Ommund Jansen Langfelt,
Great-grandfather, Skipper

Skipper, I never met you.
You and your ship were swallowed
down the sea's long throat
before I came to be.
But you had already sent
your milky school of sperm
steaming shorewards
into the harbor
of Marthe Reiersdatter
where it swelled
to its own island.

I too was there—
a salty coded cell
inside a salty cell,
within and yet within
like Russian stacked
and painted dolls:
Ommund: Marthe:
Andrea: Viktor, me.
But I was not a fraction
of a minnow, until

I, too, leapt upstream
surely as a moth to fire
towards the rising

light, dazzling,
irresistible.

Madonna della Misericordia

Piero della Francesca, circa 1452

Across the room I see you, my mother, Madonna
of Mercy—the way they've made you: queen of heaven,
crowned and jeweled, in costly red.

What did He mean who made me in you, from seed
that never touched you or spilled on your white thighs,
or let escape from you one little moan of ecstasy

the world renounced because of me? So I was made of air
and breathe it still upon the world. You open your
blue cloak, fastened by a giant blood-red ruby

to shelter small-scale kneeling patrons—Borgo's
Confraternity of Brothers for whom Piero painted you—
their Madonna, my mother—with their coifed wives

and a maiden whose hair is gold as the goldleaf
background, a pale, unconsummated bride.
In Adoration they behold you, too, as virgin.

But you are my mother; you wept, not a queen
but queenly in black, to see me whipped, crowned
not with jewels—until blood ran in my eyes.

You wept to see me carry a cross too heavy,

to see me stagger, fall. You saw me on
Golgotha's hill of skulls where I was nailed to it,

then lifted to the heavens of circling crows.
You waited, and the sky darkened. Remember,
Mother, how you kept the crows away,

you helped to place my red-stained body
in this tomb, you, my mother, I,
your beloved son. Now I stand here,

half-risen. Raise your eyes and look at me,
do I dare say—Mother?—across this room
that is a world between us, the world that I

give pain as I did you, a son without profession,
believing himself a God. But your eyes look down
upon your penitents while mine must view the world

and, even though I see the constellation
of your face, I feel the darkness rise
upon the earth. I could have walked

in olive groves forever, but I chose—
Mother, did I choose?—to stay here, fading,
watching what men do, and in my name.

III. Where Love Was Said To Be

Piazza Navona In Summer

In the Piazza Navona evening comes like a reprieve.
It is the hour of the *passeggiata:* the stones
begin to cool and the noon day's emptiness now
fills with strollers swarming out of ancient
Roman hives. Their voices hum and drone.

Back and forth, and back and forth they go
the length of the piazza, while the gods
and rivers of Bernini's fountain preside
over the tourists. They sit upon the fountain's edge
and in cafes, they eat gelato of a dozen flavors.

Vendors lay out bric-a-brac on paving stones
where heat still rises. You may have a portrait
for a price, as you would like it.
The *passeggiata* lengthens to late evening.
High above this wall of limbs, voices

thickening to a cloud that rises, I hear
—but now and then—a sweet and clear, melodious
call, the warble of a bird, or flute
like notes still haunting narrow streets of Salzburg.
My feet urge me towards what my ears believe

is true. On the smaller, second fountain
a boy sits on the edge, a boy or little man
somehow misshapen, and from his askew mouth,
his only instrument, there comes a music
high above us, lonely, a song unnoticed

as some fallen creature might say *I am*. I heard
such a music once in unknown mountain villages
in Tuscany, before the noise of little guns
invaded and crescendoed and then ceased—
the birds that sang of paradise now flown, or fallen.

Going Home to Iowa

I meet the land in my throat,
its small mounds rising; I have
known each one in particular:

wet creeks crevice into throats
and rise with rain from the sky,
blurring the hopeless lilacs;

the black walnut trees
slip like apparitions
out of dark solutions.

Presence was all: it was
the white leaf of love,
my absence unredeemable,

black as the loam of the earth
now covering rowed graves
with names deep in stone,

names once my own.
I look for me everywhere
in dry grasses, in spines

of burdock which cling to me,
milkweed pods spewing down,
the insisting thistle

purple-flowered—its thorn
touches my reaching hand.
I know each weed, where it grows

as I know that the latch
on the door rejects me, rusted
and closed to me, from inside.

The Barn

Carpeted in dust and dust's sour smell, the barn
 aches with silence.
Cobwebs crisscross like abandoned fishnets.
 Moted shafts of light
fall slant on the floor and make visible
 some random straws
aged like the hair of the old, just dead.

Hay's what this high space was built for: clover,
 lavender and green
load after load pulled up into the trolley, forkful
 by forkful,
horses harvesting their own food. Their sweat
 ran in rivulets
drying dusty white, like gone-dry brackish water
 etching tributaries
over their sleek suede. The barn was cool after work.
 The barn was shade.

Winter hovered over the barn's closed world: inside
 Brown Swiss cows
colored like cream, thickening with calf, lingered
 over summer's clover,
their tongues' harsh rasp crushing stray thistles;
 yearlings' abbreviated
moos of adolescence, perfectly held ears, wet
 pebbled noses,
their eyes holding glass miniatures of summer.
 Sounds of grain

ground in jaws of horses, their great shadowed nostrils
                    swirled air
into a cavernous dark, where love was said to be,
                    if anywhere.
The horses' snorts made frosty clouds that melted in the
                    barn's darkness,
pungent with black-walnut droppings, molding now with
                    stiffened parts of harness.

Echoes navigate the barn's high ribs; there is
                    no cooing peace
of pigeons, or hay piled there like the clouds' push
                    against the sky.
Child of my child: there is only silence
                    in this kingdom
you have never seen, and yet will lose.

Leviathan

(At The Museum of Whaling in Nantucket)

I walk under the arch of a propped-up jawbone
next to baleen, scrimshaw,
antique Boston whalers and harpoons.

Iron, God said, was straw to you.
You made a shining path
in the depths of the dark ocean,
in your wake the deep boiled red.
Upon earth, there is not your like...

I'll be Jonah and enter you: pass, fearful,
into the narthex of your mouth; wander through
the high-domed space; hear, in labyrinthine altars,
an organ fugue reverberate
as your love songs shake the seas.

You'll heave me back onto the shore
when the blue intent of steel convulses you.
You'll be parted, bargained for.

I walk under your jawbone, white as marble:
a cathedral with the altar gone.
The door is all there is.

On Reading George Catlin

Black waves rippled like an endless sea
of grasses—leviathans of the prairie were
the buffalo. They seemed to move so slowly.

Volcanic vapors issued visibly
from mouths; the whites of eyes, red tongues a blur.
Black waves rippled like an endless sea

of grasses when we were a nation hardly
formed. Our commodity was fur.
The buffalo—they seemed to move so slowly

and they thwarted a society
that needed spaces where the bobcat purred.
Black waves rippled like an endless sea.

They were a forest, now without a tree;
black ripples in the grasses won't occur
from buffalo who seemed to move so slowly.

Conquer or destroy! Not one shall flee!
Now plains are crossed with engines, smoking, surly.
Black waves rippled like an endless sea
that seemed to move so slowly: the buffalo.

Black Barley, 1934

Home from school with the only "A" in spelling
he was ever to receive, Raymond Hersberg found
his mother in the barn, trying to cut the rope
stretched tight by the weight of his father's body.
Carl's own hands had smoothed that rope: he'd eased
it out, then pulled it back to spring the hay fork's
clutch of hay as it rolled down the trolley, summer-long.
By early autumn, full up to the top, there was no space
for hangings: in spring the space between the trolley
and the hay was deep.
　　　　　　　After the pies and cakes, the sandwiches
and coffee brought by women from the neighboring
farms, the Bank came in to take possession
from the dispossessed. Maria moved
white-faced among the women and sorted hopes
she'd had to mortgage from those to throw away.
She said that Carl thought his hay was good,
"nurtured, as it was, he said, by Father's and
Grandfather's bones"—that Carl had laughed—
knowing work was never ended on a farm—
at the uses you were put to when you thought
that you were finished, that Carl had wanted
to turn into clover or black barley, "something
to feed his horses," he'd said. He'd hoped
his hogs would never get him, Maria said.

Bogie's Kiss

We kids laughed when lovers
in the weekly movie kissed.
We banged chairs
crushed empty popcorn bags
to kill the sounds
and silence words
the lovers spoke
if any.

When, in Casablanca, Bogie kissed
we held our breaths
and cheered when Ingrid left,
knowing love had lost
the girl, the man.
The conquest was the game
and kissing meant the game was over
(then Bogie said
his famous words to Sam).
We were barely ten.

When we were twelve, the kisses
brought to girls our first
burning cheeks, and gave us
hopes that *she*
would keep on kissing.
Our toes dipped into a pond
of chilled spring water, our breaths
inhaled deeply into a space

round as a negative,
shaped like an "O"
that we had yet to fill.

Edward Hopper's *Girlie Show,* 1940's

Scarlet nippled girl
white skin blurring
to red whiskey dawn

in soft light could be
Venus draped could be
Madonna eyes veiled
in virtue yet flesh-
ly mother of man
half-God

half-men gather
lured farm boys
under the street lamps
who want
to cool flaming
faces between
her white moons
whiter than
their farm-capped foreheads

want their flushed lips
to touch the scarlet star
opening to receive them
to break their stone desire

then back to the farm to
find one plain and pious girl
to marry
to pay for the
dark-revealing.

Foreclosure In Hills, Iowa, 1985

—In memory of Dale and Emily Burr

Black trees stand stark against the clapboard-white,
lonely windows stare at neighbors, the pastor
and police who trample the trackless bright
snow, outside on the winter lawn.

Bearers carry Dale and Emily
down narrow stairs, the black/tan shepherd whines
and crouches; the sun glares with reddened eye
while barn cats mew and wait for milking time.

The Guernsey cows have bursting udders, Dale's
round-rumped quarter horses stomp their feet
and whinny, nervous with the shotgun's wail
and crack—like madcap thunderstorms that tear

all pomp of spring asunder. *Our Redeemer:*
You take the plow in Your hands! Plant the clover!

On Receiving The Gilman, Iowa, Community Church Bulletin, After Thirty Years

When I was there
I longed to leave.
If I could choose again
to stay or go
I would not choose to stay
but keep my longing to return,
my heart's humming
through the open door
where I saw Christ coming
through the burning cornfields
on His way.

Reunion

We are driving down a road of the past
Don't get off, you say.
The road went on.

My hand touches your cheek.
I drew a map of the world on it. With your finger
you traced a road not taken.

That was long ago. You left

no fingerprint on my cheek
but on the body of my memory there are,

indelibly, prints like hands
so clear
the whorls of your fingers show.

The Return of Canada Geese

I have been sitting at my desk
all day, thinking of
beauty, of how to
describe it if one knows
it's there,
thinking of existence
without it,
wondering if existence
is only description.

All I have found
is a hunger
and a thirst,
unsated,
unslaked.

I should begin
with a curve of the wind,
the flared nostrils of a horse
running,
the anguish of a crying gull.

Now hear this:
it is true!
When the wing-whirr
of twelve wings
braked past my window
to one known inch
of their global world,

spring, which was only
a remembered promise
began, and I
put away my pen.

The Tomato

in memory of Margit Reverdin

All of summer, you said, holding the tomato,
                 is inside this.
I thought summer was the falling stars
                 in August, cicadas
singing in the night, the light of fireflies
                 and the bullfrog's bellow;
how I felt the sun's hot breath upon my skin.

                 But you entered the tomato,
walked into the red sun-ball, tearing open
                 its thick, burnished skin.
Inside, the green and liquid sea (like your eyes)
                 had ganglions of light
seeming all disorder, but a plan unseen
                 gave shape—inside fleshy walls
it seeded polka dots like stars,
                 fixed, but scattered in the Milky Way.

                 Its pungency wasn't
like the flowers, like plums, pears or any fruit
                 of summer, but expectant
as we feel a bee before it stings—it awes the lips,
                 startles the tongue,
piques the corners of the mouth before it sings.

Now, summer is replaced by Death outside:
                 a blue-bone cold, a stillness—
white; inside, the hiss of steam in peeling radiators.

Through this ice
I see your green-and-golden liquid eyes.
Things now commonplace were once undone
                    by names: Poisonous
Night Shade. *Paradies Apfel*. The Fruit Forbidden.

George Sand To Frederic Chopin, In Majorca

We are both expatriates:
I of my sex,
you of your country.
Now we have fled the ranting tongues of our countrymen
and here in the cool white rooms
seek shelter from the vicious sun
where I become, again, a woman.

But you have brought your country with you!
The inky cobalt of the Majorcan sky
meets and marries with the sea;
stones outline a presence sharply,
they rut the horizon,
cut the sky.

You see a muted landscape
misted with the rain of Zelazowa Wola
flattened by the glassy rivers of Mazuria.
Wind in the orange blossoms
you make into a dance of willows
and of your sisters—moving above the pools' eyes
by the River Bzura.
Bougainvillea cascading down sun-dazzled walls
turns white in your eyes
becomes the interlacing of snow
with the arms of the lilac branch
while the strings' sounds from your white room
command the sea to eternal longing,

filling the cool whiteness with the redness
of your blood, swelling the notes of your Polonaises.

"Guns covered with flowers," Schumann said.

I repatriate my sex.

Who was it that returned your Polish heart
in its urn to Poland, to the Church of the Holy Cross
in Warsaw, and walled it up
in the column of the left aisle?

Daffodils

for Ann Rosenthal on her 80th birthday

These yellow trumpets,
frilly skirts, turn upwards.
offering themselves shamelessly.
No idiots, these girls.
Cocksure and totally lacking
modesty, the whole host
of them, who can
hold them back?
       Appearance
is on their faces.
They will use it all, brazenly,
and winter will not chill them
but keep them warm
and they will wait
knowing in their sleep
that appearance is certain
and is everything.

Symbiosis

The snow has rotted—
I stagger out, light-blinded—
my foot makes a black hole in winter.
I see a white trail, jet-iced in blue sky,
of people going somewhere,
to another country, maybe.
Darkness is where my feet go.

Black trees shiver. Shrug.
They tell me nothing.
I stand here,
all motion frozen,
my foot in the black hole
of what I know. It is easier
to stand still than go anywhere.

But my feet are impatient with me.
It is too soon, I tell them,
to lay bare my gloved fingers
and move their cold touch
under the curled needles of pine.
The sodden oak leaves still carry their heaviness,
my feet their own unleavened weight.

Still, there is no stopping either of us:
the stirred ganglia trailing each other
through moss, soft on these unforgiving rocks,
among patches graced with earth warming, sharing
the leftover leaves.
                    We go creeping, sending out

last year's messages to each other.
My hand obeys, naked, feeling its way,
runs along hairy, wind-toughened nerves,
finds the cow-tongued rasp of survived leaves:
spring's first cry speeds up my arm,
informs my nose—the pungently singing breath
of the trailing arbutus.

Printed in the United States
37368LVS00006B/94-192